CW01512586

Original title:
Rugged Horns Beyond the Unicorn Fell

Copyright © 2025 Swan Charm

Author: Linda Leevike
ISBN HARDBACK: 978-1-80562-714-2
ISBN PAPERBACK: 978-1-80564-235-0

Mysteries Beneath the Age-Old Stone

Beneath the stone, where shadows creep,
Secrets slumber, lost in sleep.
Ancient voices, softly sing,
Echoes of a forgotten spring.

Graven glyphs and tales untold,
Whispers weave, both warm and cold.
In twilight's gaze, the past unfolds,
Guardians watching, shy yet bold.

With every breath, the legends sway,
Tales of night, and dusk's ballet.
From hidden depths, they rise anew,
Mysteries, timeless, deep and true.

Dawn's Light on the Stony Path

The stony path wakes with the dawn,
Golden light like lace is drawn.
Softly painted, the morning sky,
Whispers of dreams that flutter by.

Each step leads to tales unheard,
In silence, waits a fluttering bird.
Puzzles wrapped in dewdrops gleam,
Where hope and the sun entwine and dream.

Over hills, the shadows flee,
Blessings found by those who see.
So tread with care and eyes wide bright,
For every stone can spark delight.

Celestial Horns in Hidden Valleys

In valleys deep where silence sighs,
Celestial horns summon the skies.
The music weaves through fragrant air,
A call to wander, bold and rare.

Amongst the trees, the starlight sings,
As night descends on jeweled wings.
The spirits rise with every note,
In darkness, hope will always float.

The rivers dance with silver gleam,
Reflecting every whispered dream.
The secrets held in nature's clasp,
In hidden valleys, dreams enwrap.

With every horn that sounds anew,
The heart expands, the sky turns blue.
Embrace the magic, feel the tune,
Beneath the watching, gleaming moon.

The Dance of Shadows and Light

In twilight's embrace where shadows lay,
The dance of light begins to play.
With every flicker, dreams arise,
In silver beams that touch the skies.

The world transforms, a canvas bright,
As shadows twirl and take to flight.
In secret corners, stories spin,
Where night unfolds, and dreams begin.

As lanterns glow and whispers weave,
The heart believes what eyes perceive.
In harmony, they twine and sway,
The dance of night, alive, at bay.

Through every pulse and gentle breath,
The rhythm speaks of life and death.
In shadows deep, in beams so fine,
We find the truth that intertwines.

Grit and Grace of the Celestial Spire

Amidst the clouds, the spire stands,
A testament to dreams and plans.
With grit that shapes each stone and hour,
Its grace blooms bright, a vibrant flower.

Echoes of whispers, tales unique,
Of wanderers lost, of voices meek.
Each step upon the jagged stairs,
Reveals the heart's deep, hidden snares.

The winds that howl, the storms that rage,
Carve pathways that no man can gauge.
Yet hope is found in every sigh,
For light endures, though shadows lie.

A dance of stars in night's embrace,
Illuminates this sacred place.
With every twist, each daring climb,
We etch our stories against time.

So mark the heights with laughter's glee,
For in our hearts, we dare to be.
In grit combined with grace's song,
We find the strength to carry on.

Tales from the Craggy Heights

High above in rugged lands,
Where mossy rocks hold ancient strands,
Stories whisper on the breeze,
Of bold adventurers, proud as trees.

Each crag and crevice, each wild tale,
Speaks of journeys that prevail.
The echoes of both joy and woe,
Are seeds of wisdom yet to sow.

The sun sets low, the shadows play,
As twilight weaves the end of day.
Through trials faced, and bonds that grown,
A heart has strength, when truly known.

With every step on shifting stone,
A spirit forged, in light's full shone.
These heights may challenge, twist and bend,
Yet in our tales, we find a friend.

So gather round, and listen close,
To craggy tales, we cherish most.
In every story, rich and bright,
Lives courage born of craggy heights.

Legends Carved in Stone and Silence

In velvet night where shadows creep,
Legends slumber, still and deep.
Each stone holds secrets, ages past,
Whispering softly, shadows cast.

Time weaves stories, strong, discreet,
In silence deep, where echoes meet.
With every crack and every line,
Histories fade, then brightly shine.

Beneath the moon's soft silver gaze,
The ancients dance in subtle ways.
Their whispered words, like stardust flow,
In silent reverie, they bestow.

From mountains high to valleys low,
These legends teach us what we know.
With every heartbeat, every breath,
We carve our own, defying death.

So let us honor stone and night,
With tales of love, of loss, of light.
In silence there, where legends moan,
We walk the path, no longer alone.

The Dance of Starlit Antlers

Beneath the arch of twilight skies,
Where starlight weaves its shimmering ties,
The antlers sway like trees in dance,
A graceful meeting, pure romance.

Each flicker twinkles, bright and bold,
As stories of the night unfold.
In whispered breezes, secrets share,
Of woodland creatures caught midair.

With every leap, the shadows sway,
In harmony, they find their way.
Illumined by the moons' soft glow,
They paint the night, a cosmic show.

Antlers twirl in rhythmic grace,
A ballet in this sacred space.
In every flick and rustled leaf,
Exists the thread of joy and grief.

So heed the dance of night's embrace,
Where starlit antlers find their place.
For in this dance, beneath the dome,
We find our peace, we call it home.

The Melody of Mountain Spirits

Whispers weave through ancient trees,
In twilight's embrace, a gentle breeze.
Echoes of laughter in the cool of night,
The mountain spirits dance in moonlight.

Crickets serenade, a soothing song,
With each note, the shadows belong.
Stars twinkle in harmony above,
Nature's sweet chorus, a symphony of love.

Mists curl softly on the rugged stone,
Every whisper tells of secrets alone.
The melody rises, pure and bright,
Guiding lost travelers, a beacon of light.

Hills cradle the tunes like a soft embrace,
In valleys where dreams and magic race.
Every gust carries the tales of old,
Of bravery, adventure, and treasures untold.

So listen closely, to the rhythm of air,
Feel the pulse of wonder laid bare.
For in every rustle, every sigh,
The mountain spirits live, they never die.

Guardians of the Summit's Edge

Atop the peaks where few dare tread,
Stand guardians bold, in silence spread.
Their watchful eyes, like lanterns glow,
Protecting the dreams that wander below.

With sturdy frames chiseled by time,
They guard the secrets, the rhymes sublime.
Each stone and boulder their tales confess,
Of fleeting moments, of timelessness.

Snowflakes dance in a chilling breeze,
While whispers of legends echo through trees.
For every soul that climbs so high,
Finds solace where earth meets the sky.

Clouds weave around in a shroud of white,
Hiding mysteries in the still of night.
The guardians stand, ever so proud,
Untold stories wrapped in the cloud.

As dawn breaks slowly, their shadows stretch,
In golden hues, their watch they fetch.
For those who listen, and seek the song,
Will find the guardians have waited long.

The Tranquil Pulse of the Cliffs

In stillness found upon the cliffs,
Time whispers secrets like ancient myths.
Each wave that crashes, a rhythmic chime,
The cliffs' pulse matches the flow of time.

Gulls cry above in arcs so free,
As breezes carry the scent of the sea.
Rugged edges hold stories untold,
A canvas of moments in shades of gold.

Cascading waters in gentle streams,
Mirror reflections of our dreams.
Nature's heartbeat, steady and strong,
A tranquil pulse, where all belong.

Wildflowers cling to life's harsh crest,
Finding beauty where storms once pressed.
In every crevice, in every crack,
Lives a tale of courage, never lack.

So breathe in deep the strength of the earth,
Honor the cliffs for their quiet worth.
For in their embrace, peace shall reside,
A tranquil pulse, where hope and love bide.

Enchanted Shadows and Luminous Dreams

In realms where shadows softly blend,
And whispers of magic never end.
A dance of light through the forest glade,
With each fleeting moment, a memory made.

Silken fog wraps the ancient trees,
As beams of starlight tease the leaves.
In this enchanted world, time stands still,
Painting our hearts with its gentle thrill.

Dreams drift like petals upon the breeze,
Carried away to where the soul sees.
Soft lullabies hum in the night air,
Cradling wishes with tender care.

With every shadow, a story unfolds,
Of magic and wonder, of daring and bold.
The ethereal glow leads the way,
Through fields of dreams where hearts want to stray.

So chase the enchantment, let spirits soar,
For luminous dreams rest at night's door.
In shadows and light, we forever shall find,
The essence of magic, eternal and kind.

Shadows on the Skyscape

Above the world, the shadows play,
In whispers soft, they dance away.
They spin between the stars' embrace,
A fleeting trace in boundless space.

Beneath the glow of twilight's sigh,
The secrets flicker, drift, and fly.
A tapestry of night unfurls,
In shadowed hues, the sky twirls.

With every breath, the echoes blend,
As shadows stretch and gently bend.
They cloak the dreams of those who dare,
To wander realms beyond compare.

In silver beams, the moons conspire,
To light the path of dark desire.
With starlit bolts, the skies entwine,
In whispered vows, our fates align.

As dawn approaches, shadows flee,
Yet hold the night's sweet mystery.
Forever etched in hearts they dwell,
In the dawn's light, we bid farewell.

Reverie of the Tempest

In tempest's roar, the heart will race,
As winds collide and tides embrace.
The clouds gather, a battle hymn,
In nature's grip, the lights grow dim.

With rolling thunder, dreams take flight,
Amidst the storm, there's fierce delight.
Lightning paints the skies aflame,
Each strike a spark that calls my name.

The ocean's pulse sings wild and free,
In chaos lies the heart of glee.
With every wave, a story told,
Of ancient gods and treasures bold.

Yet in the storm, there's peace concealed,
A softer world, its fate revealed.
When fury calms, the waves shall part,
And in the stillness, find the heart.

The clouds will lighten, skies will clear,
And in their glow, I hold you near.
In reverie, we find our grace,
As tempests fade with love's embrace.

Secrets of the Ancient Horn

In ancient woods, the whispers weave,
Of tales long past, of those who leave.
The horn of fate, with magic bound,
In echoes deep, the lost are found.

Its melodies, a haunting call,
In shadows long, like shadows fall.
A promise made to those who stray,
To guide their steps along the way.

The secrets held beneath its song,
A history where dreams belong.
With every note, a story sighs,
In wisdom held, the ancients rise.

As twilight dims, the horn will sound,
In heartbeats shared, our souls are found.
With every breath, the past ignites,
And whispers echo through the nights.

So heed the tune, and walk with care,
For ancient paths, the brave must dare.
In secrets held, our futures lie,
Beneath the stars that light the sky.

The Wild Heart of the Highlands

In rugged peaks where eagles soar,
The heart of highlands beats with lore.
With heather blooms that paint the land,
A story rich, forever grand.

Through glen and glade, the rivers rush,
In nature's arms, the spirits hush.
The whispers of the ancient stone,
Reveal the heart, where dreams are grown.

With every wind that sweeps the vale,
There's magic in the echo's tale.
A tapestry of life and fate,
In highland dance, we resonate.

The wild heart calls, in misty shrouds,
Its voice like thunder, loud and proud.
Through trials faced and joys embraced,
In every breath, the highlands traced.

So come and feel the wilden grace,
In nature's arms, our souls find place.
In highland dreams, we find our way,
With every dawn, a new display.

Hushed Stories of the Cresting Hill

Whispers ride the evening breeze,
Softly telling tales of trees.
The shadows dance with ancient grace,
Embracing all within this place.

Stars emerge with silver light,
As day turns gently into night.
Each rustle holds a memory dear,
In hushed stories, crystal clear.

Moonlit paths begin to weave,
Secrets in the night believe.
The cresting hill, a world apart,
Where echoes cradle every heart.

Upon the journey, feet set free,
With every step, a symphony.
Nature's song, a beckoning call,
Hushed stories whisper—come, enthrall.

Once forgotten, now reborn,
In twilight's glow, a magic sworn.
And as the night begins to spill,
We find our peace upon the hill.

Beneath the Canopy of Dreams

In the forest's gentle sway,
Where light and shadow dance and play.
Beneath the leaves, a hidden world,
A tapestry of dreams unfurled.

Murmurs linger in the air,
Filling hearts with tender care.
Each sigh of wind a lullaby,
As wishes float and softly fly.

Lost within this sacred space,
We find the warmth of each embrace.
In weaving threads of hope and light,
Beneath the canopy of night.

Glimmers of magic softly gleam,
In whispers caught, we dare to dream.
The stars above our fervent guide,
Within this spell, we shall abide.

And as the dawn begins to break,
The world awakens with each shake.
Yet in our hearts, forever stays,
The dreams we kept, the magic ways.

The Enigma of the Furrowed Facade

A face of stone with tales untold,
In furrowed lines, a heart of old.
What mysteries in silence hide,
Behind the mask, a soul inside?

Each crease a lesson, harsh and wise,
Reflecting years beneath the skies.
With every wrinkle, stories bloom,
Of laughter, love, and shadowed gloom.

In twilight's glow, the truths uncoil,
Of sunlit days and midnight toil.
The enigma beckons, strange and bold,
A portrait rich, in whispers sold.

A tapestry of joy and strife,
Weaving through the fabric of life.
In every furrow, echo sings,
The wisdom worn from life's deep springs.

So let us linger, gaze and find,
The beauty hidden, intertwined.
For in this facade, a spark we see,
The essence of our mystery.

Elysian Wildflowers in Serpentines

In fields where colors freely bloom,
Wildflowers dance in sweet perfume.
Elysian dreams in petals bright,
A canvas woven, pure delight.

Winding paths, like whispers go,
Through valleys rich with sunlit glow.
Each blossom tells of tales anew,
In every hue, a moment true.

The breeze carries laughter as it sways,
In gentle arcs and sunlight's rays.
S serpentine, the journeys bend,
Where nature's notes and hearts transcend.

Among the blooms, a fleeting chance,
In every step, we find a dance.
With every breath, the magic twines,
In elysian wildflowers' signs.

So roam these paths of nature's song,
Where hearts align and dreams belong.
In the fields of joy, we shall stay,
And let our spirit guide the way.

Dreams of the Celestial Herd

In twilight's grasp, the skies unfold,
The whispered tales of stars of old.
Across the fields of silent gleam,
The celestial herd wades through a dream.

With hooves that dance on silver light,
They weave their paths through endless night.
Each galaxy, a world untamed,
In cosmic essence, wild and famed.

They leap through realms of time and fate,
In majestic arcs, they celebrate.
The moon their guide, the sun their shield,
In the celestial chase, they never yield.

Through fields of stardust, secrets blend,
This ethereal race will never end.
They chase the echoes of wishes long,
In dreams of night, forever strong.

Echoes of the Ancient Trailblazers

In valleys deep where shadows dwell,
The echoes of the past do swell.
Trailblazers brave, with hearts aglow,
They paved the paths that we now know.

With each footfall, a story's told,
Of silent whispers, bold and old.
They journeyed forth with spirits bright,
Guided by the stars at night.

Through rivers wide and mountains steep,
Their legacies in memories sleep.
Resilient souls, they paved the way,
For dreamers lost, to find their sway.

In every breath of breezy air,
The essence of their courage, rare.
A bond with earth that's forged in fire,
Their echoes fuel the heart's desire.

Murmurs from the Ridge of Legends

Upon the ridge, where legends stand,
Murmurs rise from the ancient land.
The winds weave tales of glory past,
Of heroes forged, their shadows cast.

With echoes soft as twilight's sigh,
Their whispers float through the dusky sky.
Each stone a witness, each tree a sage,
In nature's tale, they turn the page.

The mountains cradle their memories near,
In every gust, their voices clear.
Bravery carved in the heart of stone,
Lives forever, never alone.

From dawn till dusk, their spirits roam,
In every corner, they call it home.
On silent nights, when stars align,
The ridge of legends, forever divine.

The Celestial Trail of the Brave

In the realm where dreams take flight,
The brave carve paths through endless night.
Each step, a spark of hope and fire,
The celestial trail, their hearts inspire.

Through constellations, they boldly tread,
On unknown roads, where few have led.
The cosmos calls with a whisper sweet,
A journey grand that can't be beat.

With starlit guides and skies so wide,
They find their strength in every stride.
In every heartbeat, a tale is spun,
The trail of the brave has just begun.

So let them soar on wings of grace,
In galaxies vast, they find their place.
With courage as their guiding light,
They walk the path, through day and night.

The Heartbeat of Untamed Nature

In forests deep where shadows play,
The whispered winds in wild ballet.
Each leaf a story, every stone,
A heartbeat sings, the wild alone.

With rustling grass and splashing streams,
Nature's canvas holds our dreams.
A symphony of life unfolds,
In vibrant hues, a tale retold.

Beneath the stars, the night ascends,
The moonlight dances, magic bends.
Creatures stir with gentle grace,
In this untouched, enchanted space.

The mountains rise, both grand and bold,
Their ancient roots, a tale of old.
While rivers carve the path of time,
In nature's heart, we find our rhyme.

So let us wander, hearts set free,
In nature's arms, our spirits glee.
With every breath, we feel the charm,
The heartbeat of the wild, our balm.

In the Twilight of Forgotten Realms

In twilight's hush, the secrets bloom,
Where shadows linger, drawing gloom.
Forgotten tales in whispers weave,
A tapestry of time, we cleave.

The echo of a distant song,
In realms where dreams can drift along.
With every sigh of evening's breath,
A dance with echoes born of death.

The stars align, a guiding light,
In this realm of fading night.
Phantoms flicker, shapes that sway,
As time stretches, pulls away.

A castle lost in verdant glades,
With ivy woven through the shades.
Within its walls, a ghostly waltz,
Where hope and memory never faults.

So tread softly on the veil,
For here, the past begins to frail.
In twilight's grip, we find a thread,
Connecting worlds with words unsaid.

Songbirds Over Stony Moors

Amidst the heather, a songbird trills,
Its melody a balm for hills.
Over stony moors, they glide,
Nature's chorus, wild and wide.

The misty air and morning dew,
Each note a dance, each echo true.
With wings that brush the sky so blue,
In flight, their freedom we pursue.

The rugged stones, they stand as shields,
Guarding the stories that nature yields.
As songbirds weave through air so light,
They fill the dawn with pure delight.

Through valleys deep and hills that rise,
Their serenade claims twilight skies.
While shadows stretch and daylight fades,
Their songs enchant, the beauty wades.

So let us wander, hearts alight,
Where songbirds sing and dreams take flight.
In harmony with earth's embrace,
We find our peace, our sacred space.

The Twilight Dance of the Elusive

In twilight's glow, the shadows sway,
A dance of forms begins to play.
The elusive wraiths of dreamer's lore,
Step softly on the forest floor.

Their whispers float like fleeting mist,
In silver strands of night, they twist.
With every spark, a glimmer bright,
The dance unfolds, a secret rite.

As stars ignite the velvet sky,
Elusive beings twirl and fly.
Their laughter rings through tangled trees,
A melody that rides the breeze.

In stolen moments, magic brews,
With every step, the heart renews.
Through gentle movements, they invite,
The world to join in this delight.

So tread with care, yet feel the call,
For in this dance, we are enthralled.
The twilight beckons, come and see,
The elusive waltz, set spirit free.

The Call of the Wild Lyric

In the forest deep, where shadows play,
Whispers of the wild beckon, sway.
Every leaf and twig, a tale to weave,
Nature's song, to believe, to believe.

The river sings of ancient lore,
With every ripple, secrets galore.
Step softly, listen to the breeze,
For it carries stories with such ease.

Beneath the moon, the creatures hide,
Actors on a stage, with wild pride.
Stars above twinkle in delight,
As night unfolds its cloak of light.

A howl breaks free, a call so clear,
Echoes through the woods, far and near.
The wild awakens, a stirring heart,
In every creature, a vital part.

So venture forth, take heed and tread,
Where dreams and nightmares fear to spread.
For in the wild, you'll find your spark,
Illuminating paths through the dark.

Fables Across the Fractured Skies

Beneath the veil of fractured stars,
Lies a world of whispers, dreams, and scars.
Tales of old hang in the air,
Carried by the winds, so rare, so rare.

Voices of ancients, soft and sweet,
Entwine like vines, a rhythmic beat.
They speak of hope, of love, of loss,
In shadows cast by a world embossed.

The moonlight dances on silver streams,
Each ripple holds a thousand dreams.
Listen closely, the night reveals,
Magic in the dark, a fate that feels.

Across the heavens, stories soar,
Boundless words that forever explore.
Legends etched in time's embrace,
Threaded through the endless space.

So gaze aloft, let your heart fly,
In the tapestry of night's high sigh.
For every star, a tale unfolds,
In the fables that the cosmos holds.

Twilight's Embrace on Jagged Cliffs

At dusk, the cliffs stand proud and tall,
Kissed by the sun's last golden call.
The ocean roars with timeless grace,
Cascading dreams to the wild place.

A solitary bird takes flight,
Carving stories in the soft twilight.
Each gust of wind, a gentle nudge,
Calls forth the night with a tender grudge.

In shadows deep, secrets lie,
Whispered tales to the starry sky.
The rocks breathe history, ancient and wise,
Worn by the tides beneath the skies.

With every wave that crashes bold,
Echoes of love and sorrow unfold.
In twilight's clutch, the world feels right,
As dreams arise with the onset of night.

So linger long on the jagged edge,
Where earth and sky come to pledge.
For in that space, hearts will yearn,
In twilight's embrace, we still return.

Chronicles of the Celestial Grove

In the grove where stars entwine,
Ancient spirits in silence shine.
Leaves whisper secrets, forgotten lore,
Echoes of magic, forevermore.

Each tree a keeper, wise and grand,
Rooted deep in the elder's hand.
The moonlight laces through boughs wide,
Casting dreams where the lost confide.

A spark ignites in darkened glades,
Flickering hopes in shadowed shades.
Listen close to the flowing stream,
For it carries the wishes of a dream.

The constellations guide the way,
Painting paths where the heart can sway.
In this celestial expanse so bright,
Find your place 'neath the quilt of night.

So wander forth, let spirits guide,
Through the grove where wonders reside.
For in the chronicles, truth is spun,
A tapestry woven, never undone.

Chronicles of the Celestial Herd

In twilight's glow, they gather near,
Horns aglow with starlit cheer.
Through whispering woods, they weave and roam,
The spirits of the night call them home.

With every hoof, tales unfold,
Of ancient magic, brave and bold.
They dance in circles, a celestial ring,
Beneath the moon, their voices sing.

Across the hills, a shimmered grace,
Time stands still in this sacred space.
Each heartbeat echoes with purpose clear,
In the heart of the wild, they persevere.

Upon the winds, their legends soar,
Whispers echo from shore to shore.
In twilight's glow, they seek the light,
The Celestial Herd, in endless flight.

Gather, dear friend, come see the sight,
As dreams take form on this starry night.
With tales long cherished, secrets shared,
In the chronicles where few have dared.

Phantoms of the High Ledge

Upon the edge where shadows dwell,
Phantoms weave their haunting spell.
Whispers haunt the mossy stone,
Echoes of the past, forever known.

In misty veils, their forms appear,
Figures dancing, never near.
Reveal your truth, oh shades of yore,
What tales from yesterday's core?

The ledge remembers, steep and wide,
Secrets buried where dreams abide.
Gentle breezes carry cries,
Of lost loves, of endless goodbyes.

Cloaked in silence, they linger still,
Guardians of the forgotten hill.
Their sorrowed song, a mournful plea,
Drifting on winds, forever free.

So heed the call of the high ledge,
Where phantoms dance upon the edge.
For in their whispers, we may find,
The stories entwined in heart and mind.

Glories of the Mountain's Assert

Among the peaks where eagles soar,
Glimmers show what dreams restore.
A kingdom rises, rough yet grand,
The mountain holds its mighty stand.

With every climb, a story shared,
Of trials faced and burdens bared.
In crests the sun sets, painting gold,
A tapestry of marvels told.

Through snow and stone, the winds proclaim,
The glories stitched within its name.
A dance of light on rugged stone,
The mountain's heart beats, fiercely known.

Beneath its shadow, dreams take flight,
Guided by the stars so bright.
With every step up craggy height,
The mountain calls, a gentle might.

So climb and seek what lies in wait,
Gaze upon the mountain's gate.
In its embrace, the world appears,
A testament through all the years.

Secrets of the Highland Echoes

In valleys deep, where echoes hide,
The secrets of the Highland glide.
Songs of old in whispered tones,
Carried through the ancient stones.

The river flows with stories grand,
Of clans and kin, of freedom's stand.
Where laughter danced in dusk's embrace,
And love once bloomed, a sacred space.

The echoes blend with nature's breath,
Roots entwined in life and death.
Each note a tale, a fleeting glance,
Of whispered hope in every chance.

So listen close, the highland sings,
Revealing all that nature brings.
Beneath the stars, let visions grow,
In the secrets that the highland knows.

Breathe in the past, let silence weave,
The threads of dreams that we believe.
For in this land, with every beat,
The echoes hum, a soft retreat.

Heartbeats in the Mystical Stillness

In quiet groves where whispers dwell,
The magic stirs, a soft-spun spell.
Beneath the ancient oaken trees,
A dance of light upon the breeze.

With every pulse the night draws near,
While starlit skies erase our fear.
A heartbeat's echo, faint yet bold,
Guides us to secrets long untold.

The moon reflects on silver streams,
Where dreams awaken, bright as beams.
Each glance reveals the hidden paths,
Where nature's voice to silence hath.

In stillness deep, our hearts align,
With throbbing rhythm, pure divine.
In every breath, the world stands still,
Embracing traits of ancient will.

As twilight fades and shadows creep,
The echoes of our dreams we keep.
In mystical realms, our spirits soar,
As heartbeats draw us evermore.

The Fables of Stone and Wind

In valleys low where echoes rise,
The winds tell tales beneath the skies.
Of mountains steep and rivers wide,
The stones will weep for what they hide.

With every gust, the past unfolds,
In whispered words, the saga holds.
A hero's path, a hero's woe,
In nature's breath, the fables flow.

The ancient trees, in murmur soft,
Bear witness to the dreams aloft.
The stones, they sing of time gone by,
With every breeze, a mournful sigh.

Each crag and cliff, a silent plea,
Of battles fought and victory.
The wind, the keeper of the lore,
Guides wandering spirits evermore.

As dusk arrives, the tales entwine,
In shadows cast, the stars align.
The fables born of stone and air,
Whisper their truths for those who dare.

Shadows Linger in the Highland Mist

In fading light, the mist will weave,
A tapestry none would believe.
Where shadows dance and secrets sigh,
In verdant glens, the spirits fly.

The heather blooms in purple hue,
While whispers float like morning dew.
Each winding path, a tale concealed,
In nature's heart, the truth revealed.

Oft in the dusk, a haunting tune,
Calls forth the velvet cloak of moon.
In hidden nooks, the shadows play,
A symphony at close of day.

A breath of wind, a fleeting shade,
In every heart, a truth displayed.
With every step, the echoes call,
In Highland mist, we find it all.

As night descends, the world holds fast,
To stories woven from the past.
In shadows deep, we come to see,
The whispers guide our destiny.

The Flight of the Ethereal One

On feathered wings, the spirit soars,
Through realms unknown, on open doors.
With grace it dances through the air,
In every glance, a silent prayer.

From mountain high to valleys low,
The winds of change begin to blow.
A spark of light in twilight's glow,
The ethereal one shall surely flow.

With eyes that twinkle like the stars,
It whispers secrets from afar.
In twilight's grasp, it weaves a tale,
Of love and hope that will not pale.

To follow where the heart is drawn,
Through shadows cast, beyond the dawn.
The flight is wild, yet gentle too,
A journey grand for me and you.

As dawn breaks clear and skies unfold,
The stories old and new retold.
In flight we find the threads of fate,
The ethereal one can never wait.

Above the Misty Horizon of Dreams

Beneath the skies of endless blue,
Where wishes dance and spirits flew,
The whispers call from heights unknown,
In twilight's glow, our hearts are sown.

We chase the light on paths of gold,
With stories waiting to be told,
Each star above a guiding spark,
As shadows flicker in the dark.

Through valleys deep and mountains high,
The dreams unfurl and gently sigh,
With every step, a glimpse persists,
Above the mist where hope exists.

In every heart, a daring spark,
To dance with tales that leave their mark,
The journey stirs a fervent flame,
In whispered winds, we find our names.

So take my hand, let's wander far,
Where moonlit paths and wonders are,
Together lost, yet ever found,
Above the mist, our dreams abound.

Where the Ethereal Creatures Roam

In glades enchanted, shadows glide,
Where secret beings shyly hide,
With wings of gossamer so bright,
They weave the threads of day and night.

The whispered echoes of the trees,
Sing songs that dance upon the breeze,
A world where magic gently hums,
And every heart to wonder succumbs.

Beneath the glow of lunar beams,
They flit like stardust in our dreams,
With glimmering eyes, they take their flight,
Through realms of shadow, and pure light.

In gentle gatherings, they play,
Where worries fade, and fears decay,
Together lost in joy's embrace,
In every form, their grace leaves trace.

So wander forth where wonders bloom,
Among these spirits, cast away gloom,
For in their realm of pure delight,
The heart finds joy, a rarest sight.

Secrets of the Untamed Highlands

Through rugged hills, the echoes call,
Of ancient tales, both great and small,
In whispers lost to time and stone,
The highlands guard their secrets lone.

With winds that sweep the heathered lands,
And skies that stretch with gentle hands,
The stones remember all that's past,
In every shadow, shadows cast.

A path of dreams through twilight weaves,
Where every heart the wildness leaves,
Beneath the gaze of starlit eyes,
The spirit dances, never cries.

In every brook and mountain high,
The wonders breathe, they never die,
In laughter and in aged sighs,
The secrets flow like timeless skies.

So wander forth, embrace the wild,
Find solace there, like a lost child,
For in the highlands, truth will gleam,
In every heart, a whispered dream.

Heartbeats of the Midnight Mountains

In twilight's hush, the mountains rise,
With silent strength and watchful sighs,
A symphony of stars unfolds,
As night reveals its secrets bold.

The shadows dance on rugged stone,
Where whispers cradle the unknown,
Each heartbeat thunders like a drum,
In the embrace of night, we come.

The cool winds bring a tale to share,
Of echoes lost in midnight air,
Through craggy paths and skies so wide,
The mountains hold what dreams confide.

With every step, the world will change,
Within the dark, the wild and strange,
A promise made by moonlit grace,
In undying peace, we find our place.

So hear the call, in stars we trust,
Where mountains' heartbeat turns to dust,
In midnight's arms, we climb and soar,
To find the dreams we all adore.

Chasing the Clouds at Dusk

The sun dips low, with golden rays,
Painting the sky in vibrant displays.
Whispers of twilight beckon dreams,
As shadows dance in silken gleams.

On broomstick rides through lavender air,
We chase our hopes, shedding despair.
With laughter bright, we twirl and spin,
In the twilight, where magic begins.

The clouds, like ships, sail slow and bold,
Carrying secrets yet untold.
Every breath, a spell we weave,
In the dusk, we choose to believe.

Stars awaken in the violet hue,
Guiding our hearts to what is true.
In the hush of twilight's embrace,
We find our dreams in this hidden place.

So chase the clouds, let spirits soar,
In the twilight, seek forevermore.
Through mysteries of dusk, we'll glide,
Together, side by side, we bide.

Hooves of Myth on Grassy Knolls

In fields of green, where stories sleep,
Hooves of legend through silence creep.
Glimmers of silver, tails that fly,
Creatures of wonder pass us by.

Beneath the boughs of ancient trees,
Echoes of tales drift on the breeze.
Fairies and fables, wild and free,
In grassy knolls, they call to me.

Each hoofbeat drums a timeless song,
In secret glens where dreams belong.
With every stride, the earth awakes,
As shadows dance in twilight's makes.

Nature's whispers, soft and clear,
Invite the heart to bend the ear.
In twilight's grace, we lose our fears,
Carried away on the winds of years.

So heed the call of mythic lore,
And let your spirit ever soar.
For in those knolls where legends play,
Magic resides in night and day.

Beyond the Mystic Glade

In the heart of woods, where shadows blend,
A mystic glade calls, where dreamers wend.
With glimmering light that plays and sways,
It whispers of wonder in secret ways.

Through tangled roots and silver streams,
The air is thick with moonlit dreams.
A place where wishes drift like leaves,
And the heart finds hope, while the spirit believes.

The fae dance lightly on petals rare,
Their laughter mingling with scented air.
In captivating hues, they twirl and spin,
Inviting lost souls to dance within.

A soft breeze carries a timeless tongue,
Twisting stories of the old and young.
Through glades enchanted, we weave our fate,
In the arms of magic, we contemplate.

So wander forth into the sublime,
Embrace the magic woven through time.
Beyond the glade, where dreams hold sway,
A world of wonder, forever will stay.

The Call of the Untouched Wild

In the heart of the wild, where nature breathes,
Untamed whispers sway the trembling leaves.
Mountains stand tall, like guards of yore,
Holding the secrets of ages before.

The rivers sing with a crystal grace,
Inviting wanderers to leave their trace.
Through emerald forests, wildflowers bloom,
In the untouched wild, there's room to groom.

A symphony blares in the softest tones,
The call of freedom, where the wild roams.
Sitting and listening, we hear the call,
Of the mountains, the rivers, embracing us all.

With every heartbeat, the world aligns,
In the untouched wild, a love that shines.
So take a step into the wild spree,
Where every breath is a song, wild and free.

Let the wild beckon, open your heart,
As nature's beauty plays its part.
For in that call, our spirits rest,
In the untouched wild, we find our best.

Memories Carved in Time

In quiet corners, shadows play,
The echoes of laughter drift away.
Soft whispers linger, tales unfold,
As dreams unfurl like threads of gold.

Through the misty veil of yesteryears,
Time dances lightly, shedding tears.
Each fading photograph we hold dear,
A testament to love, lost yet near.

In secret gardens, flowers bloom,
They carry stories, dispelling gloom.
With every petal that falls like rain,
Memories linger, both joy and pain.

The old oak stands, a guardian wise,
Witness to laughter and whispered sighs.
Through seasons of change, it remains strong,
A sentinel to the forgotten song.

Here in the silence, time stands still,
Each heartbeat echoes, a gentle thrill.
With eyes closed tight, we journey wide,
To find the treasures that time can't hide.

Lanterns of Forgotten Routes

In the twilight glow, soft lanterns sway,
Guiding lost souls along their way.
Each flickering light a story told,
Of paths once walked, of dreams turned bold.

Beneath the stars, shadows intertwine,
A tapestry woven through space and time.
With whispers of wind, the roads we trace,
Reveal the secrets of this enchanted place.

Old cobbled streets, lost in the night,
Speak of travelers, hearts full of light.
Each step we take, a borrowed grace,
As lanterns dance with a ghostly face.

In the stillness, the echoes call,
A beckoning voice from the heart of it all.
We wander forth with courage anew,
Embracing the magic, the wild, the true.

With every turn, the journey unfolds,
The lanterns flicker, their secrets behold.
A symphony woven through dreams and fears,
Guides us onward through laughter and tears.

The Weaver's Tale in the Sierras

In mountain air where eagles soar,
A weaver spins tales of ancient lore.
With nimble fingers, the threads unite,
Crafting the essence of day and night.

Through fragrant forests and rivers clear,
Each woven strand whispers, 'I am here.'
Colors entwine in vibrant hues,
A testament to heart's quiet muse.

The loom is a canvas, vast and wide,
Stories of wanderers who once confide.
Beneath the stars, the patterns gleam,
Bringing to life each distant dream.

The mountains echo with laughter bright,
As memories weave in the soft twilight.
With every stitch, the weaver binds
The hopes and dreams of countless minds.

In a sanctuary of cliffs so steep,
The weaver's tale is ours to keep.
In every fiber, a story spun,
Embracing the many, uniting as one.

Whispers from the Forgotten Promontory

Atop the cliffs where seagulls cry,
Whispers of ages drift and sigh.
The ocean's breath a soothing balm,
In the midst of chaos, a world of calm.

Worn stones hold tales of those who came,
In search of solace, in search of fame.
Each footstep echoes upon the ground,
A reminder of dreams lost, yet found.

The salty winds carry secrets deep,
Of love that forged, of promises to keep.
Beneath the moon, the waves do churn,
As shadows dance and lanterns burn.

Here in the stillness, hearts entwine,
Bound by the threads of a sacred line.
As whispers linger, soft and low,
They guide our souls where we must go.

The stars above, a watchful gaze,
Illuminate paths through darkened haze.
In the hands of fate, we find our way,
To the forgotten promontory where dreams sway.

Boundless Spirit of the Untamed Realm

In a realm where shadows dance and play,
The whispers of the wild call forth the day.
Mountains rise like giants, proud and tall,
Echoes of ancient secrets weave through all.

The rivers sing a song of ages past,
Carving paths where dreams and tales are cast.
Beneath the stars, the spirit roams so free,
A glimpse into the heart of mystery.

Flora blooms with colors bright and bold,
Guarding stories waiting to be told.
The winds carry laughter through the trees,
Nurturing the magic, stirring the breeze.

Creatures of the night in shadows glide,
With eyes like lanterns, hiding fate inside.
Together they weave nature's wondrous spell,
Where every heartbeat resonates and dwells.

In the vast expanse, where dreams unite,
Boundless is the spirit, a guiding light.
In every rustling leaf, in every sound,
The untamed realm awakens, unbound.

Dreams Woven in Nature's Canvas

Upon the canvas of the dawn's first glow,
Nature spills her colors, bright and slow.
Each petal, each blade, a story shared,
In the tapestry of life, we are all dared.

Sunbeams dance with shadows, side by side,
Creating realms where hopes and dreams reside.
Every rustle whispers secrets of the heart,
A bond with the earth, never to part.

The brook, it glistens with laughter pure,
While time, like a gentle breeze, assures.
A canvas woven with threads of fire,
Where every moment sings of sweet desire.

The clouds drift lazily, a painter's brush,
In hues of lavender, in twilight's hush.
Underneath the vast and whispering sky,
Dreams take flight like birds, soaring high.

In quiet corners where love takes root,
Find solace among the wildflower's shoot.
With each new dawn, a promise to behold,
As nature's canvas shimmers, pure and bold.

The Siren's Song of the Rustic Wild

Through tangled woods where secrets breathe,
A siren sings, tempting hearts to believe.
Her voice, a melody soft and sweet,
Lures wanderers to where forest and river meet.

Stars twinkle above in the cosmic sea,
The call of the wild, enchanting and free.
In rustling leaves, her echoes linger,
A haunting warmth like a familiar finger.

Beneath the moon's glow, the shadows sway,
In the heart of the night, they softly play.
Each whispering breeze carries her refrain,
A timeless tale beneath the silver rain.

From the depths of the thicket, a story unfurls,
Of forgotten realms and enchanted swirls.
With every note, the wildflowers dance,
In the siren's song, all creatures entranced.

The rustic wild, where nature's heart beats,
A symphony of life, where freedom greets.
So listen closely, let your spirit roam,
For the siren's song will always lead you home.

Cresting Waves of Myth and Memory

On the edge of time where the ocean sighs,
Waves weave tales under the vast, open skies.
Each crest a memory, each trough a dream,
In the ocean's embrace, the stories gleam.

Legends rise like ships in the morning mist,
Whispers of sailors and journeys untwist.
The horizon beckons, a shimmering line,
Where myth and reality gracefully intertwine.

Footprints in the sand tell of love long lost,
Echoes of laughter, the beauty of what's tossed.
With every wave that crashes, a heart unbinds,
Sailing through time, where adventure finds.

In tides that ebb and flow like a dance,
Lies the pulse of memories, a chance.
As starlight reflects on the water's face,
In cresting waves, we find our place.

Beneath the vastness, where dreams may drift,
The ocean's whispers are a timeless gift.
In the depths of her mysteries, we find our way,
Cresting the waves of myth, day by day.

Mystic Peaks of Fabled Beasts

In the mist, they roam so free,
Guardians of the ancient tree.
With wings of night and hearts of fire,
They weave the dreams of one desire.

Beneath the stars, their shadows dance,
In moonlit glades, they take their chance.
With whispered calls, the legends soar,
A tapestry of myth once more.

Hidden paths unveil their grace,
In deep, enchanted, secret place.
Their eyes reflect the stories told,
Of quests for love and victories bold.

Each footstep echoes tales of old,
Of battles fierce, and treasures gold.
Amongst the peaks where silence reigns,
The pulse of magic still remains.

So, wander not with heart of dread,
For where they tread, no shadows spread.
Embrace the night, let spirits tease,
In mystic peaks, your heart will seize.

Whispers of the Ancient Ridge

Upon the ridge where few have gone,
Whispers rise with the dawn's first song.
Elders speak of twilight's tale,
With every breeze, their words prevail.

Time-weary stones guard secrets deep,
In silence vast, where shadows creep.
With hallowed air, the spirits sigh,
As echoes dance, and dreams fly high.

Among the trees, the past will tread,
With gentle grace, the lost are led.
In every sound the ancients tell,
Of magic spheres, of hidden wells.

So linger long, let heart be brave,
For nature's lore is meant to save.
In quiet glens, your fears release,
With every whisper, nature's peace.

And when the moon begins to rise,
Let wonder fill your searching eyes.
For on this ridge, through time's embrace,
You'll find your own enchanted place.

The Echoes of Enchanted Summits

Up high where the eagles dare to glide,
Echoes of old in twilight abide.
With every breath, the mountains sing,
The songs of all that magic brings.

Wonders wake with the break of day,
In the shimmering dew where fairies play.
With laughter bright and spirits light,
They dance through shadows, out of sight.

Hidden valleys resonate the truth,
Of lost adventures in timeless youth.
In every gaze, a story's spun,
Of battles fought, and journeys won.

These summits high speak brave and bold,
With tales of dragons, dreams retold.
In whispered tones, they share the past,
A legacy of hope to last.

So climb the height, embrace the call,
For echoes linger, love binds all.
In the magic wrought by earth and sky,
The enchanted summits wonder why.

Aria of the Fabled Heights

In shadows deep, where whispers soar,
A tale unfolds on mountains' core.
With every breath, the echoes twine,
A symphony of realms divine.

The skies adorn with shimmering light,
And stars ignite the velvet night.
With courage drawn from ancient lore,
We seek the heights forevermore.

Upon the breeze, the secrets ride,
Of battles fought and destinies tried.
The winds will sing of paths untold,
The fables etched in threads of gold.

A dance of tales on starlit streams,
Where hope awakens faded dreams.
Each heartbeat chimes in harmony,
A timeless song, forever free.

So raise your voice to skies afar,
Let legends weave, be who you are.
Embrace the song, the fabled years,
For in these heights, we cast our fears.

Shadows in the Valley of Myth

In the valley where shadows creep,
Secrets buried in silence deep.
With tales spun from the thread of night,
The myths awaken, taking flight.

Beneath the boughs of ancient trees,
Where whispers kiss the autumn breeze.
With every rustle, legends bloom,
In twilight's breath, dispelling gloom.

The moonlight weaves a silver map,
Guiding wanderers through each trap.
With echoes lost in winds of time,
The call of destiny, a chime.

In shadows cast by fleeting dreams,
The world, it dances, or so it seems.
With every heartbeat, myths revive,
In valley lore, the lost survive.

So venture forth, let not fear bind,
For in this place, the brave will find.
In the valley, where echoes dwell,
The shadows hold a magic spell.

Echoing Heartbeats of Nature

Beneath the boughs where shadows play,
The heart of nature beats away.
With every rustle, whispers call,
To wanderers brave, who heed their thrall.

The rivers sing in liquid tones,
A melody of ancient bones.
In every leaf, a story spun,
Of seasons passed, and battles won.

Through twilight woods, the echoes roam,
A sanctuary, nature's home.
The creatures stir and dance in glee,
As time unfolds its tapestry.

In hidden glades, the shadows blend,
The cycle turns, as meanings bend.
Embrace the pulse, the life within,
For nature's song will never dim.

So close your eyes, let essence flow,
In heartbeats soft, we come to know.
A world alive, in every breath,
A bond unbroken, beyond death.

Horizon's Edge and Hidden Dreams

At horizon's edge, where daylight fades,
The dreams emerge from dusky glades.
With colors rich, the canvas gleams,
Awaking hope from slumbered dreams.

The twilight whispers of what's to be,
In shadows cast, the soul flies free.
Each step we take on paths unseen,
Leads to the realms where we convene.

The stars ignite, a guiding light,
In endless journeys through the night.
With every heartbeat, promise flows,
As dreams reveal what courage shows.

In silence stitched with threads of fate,
We find the strength to navigate.
With hearts ablaze, we chase the dawn,
Embracing all that we have drawn.

So wander forth, in love we trust,
For in our dreams, we rise from dust.
At horizon's edge, we make our stand,
And carve our truth in life's vast land.

The Tapestry of Lost Legends

In chambers deep, where stories sleep,
The tapestry unfolds, secrets we keep.
With threads of time, the looms engage,
In whispers old, on history's page.

Each legend inked in shadows cast,
A portal to a long-lost past.
With every stitch, the fabric twines,
As dreams awaken, fate aligns.

The hero's journey, loved and lost,
In echoes soft, we feel the cost.
Through woven paths, the heart will seek,
For in our dreams, it dares to speak.

So gather near, let voices soar,
For in this tale, we find our lore.
The threads connect, both near and far,
Reflecting truths in every scar.

With legends claimed, and battles fought,
In every heart, a lesson taught.
Embrace the past, the whispers call,
For in this tapestry, we are all.

Whispers of the Mountain's Edge

Beneath the pines, where shadows dwell,
A tale of magic, the mountains tell.
With whispers soft, the winds do weave,
A story grand for those who believe.

Amongst the rocks, where wild things roam,
The echoes call, inviting home.
A shimmering path, with secrets old,
In every breath, adventures bold.

The stars above, a guiding light,
Through misty dreams of silent night.
Each step enchanted, the earth our stage,
With every heartbeat, we turn the page.

In twilight's grace, the shadows play,
With murmurs sweet as night turns gray.
A bond unspoken, between the trees,
The heart knows well, the wild's decrees.

So heed the call, let your spirit soar,
At the mountain's edge, forevermore.

Echoes of the Untamed Heights

Where craggy peaks kiss the sky,
The clouds are whispers, soaring high.
A symphony of wild delight,
The echoes dance in fading light.

Step softly now, where eagles glide,
Through valleys deep, where dreams abide.
The air grows thin, the heart beats slow,
In hidden glens where wildflowers grow.

The stories told by firelight's glow,
Of brave souls who dared the winds to blow.
With every step, the spirits sigh,
As ancient paths twist and lie.

A heartbeat's rhythm, the world aligns,
Through untamed heights, a path that shines.
In whispered hopes, the wilds conspire,
With every breath, we rise higher.

So tread the trails where few have walked,
In nature's presence, we are awed,
For echoes of the untamed speak,
In every rustling leaf, unique.

Starlit Paths Through Wild Meadows

Beneath the sky where dreams unfold,
The meadow glimmers, a sight to behold.
With starlit paths, we wander free,
In nature's arms, forever we'll be.

As gentle breezes whisper near,
Each blade of grass sings sweet and clear.
In wild meadows where laughter rings,
The heart finds joy that freedom brings.

With moonlight casting silvery beams,
The night awakens our sweetest dreams.
A dance of shadows, twinkling bright,
We lose ourselves in the magic's light.

The flowers sway, a vibrant show,
Their colors burst, a radiant glow.
Each step we take, the earth does sigh,
As starlit paths beckon us nigh.

So let us wander, let us roam,
In wild meadows, we find our home.
With stars as guides, we forge our way,
In nature's cradle, come what may.

The Guardian's Crest

Upon the cliffs where shadows dwell,
The guardian stands, a timeless spell.
With watchful eyes on lands below,
A silent oath, in moonlit glow.

Through storms that rage and winds that wail,
The crest remains, a steadfast tale.
In whispers soft, it calls the brave,
To seek the truth, their hearts to save.

With fables etched in stone and night,
The guardian guards with all its might.
In twilight's hush, the memories flow,
Of battles fought and love's soft glow.

From heights unseen, the world laid bare,
Each journey marked by heart and care.
A promise kept through darkest fears,
In every pulse, the path appears.

So heed the call of the guardian's crest,
For in its watch, the wild's at rest.
With open hearts, we rise and dream,
In the guardian's light, forever gleam.

Of Echoes and Enchantment

In the heart of the whispering woods,
Where shadows dance with delight,
Echoes weave tales of old,
In the moon's gentle light.

Songs of fairies and dreams,
Brought forth on the breeze,
Enchantments flicker and gleam,
With every rustle of leaves.

Secrets hidden in glades,
Awaiting the dawn's kiss,
Magic flows through the blades,
A world steeped in bliss.

Where time gently pauses,
And whispers embrace the night,
The echoes of laughter,
Spark wonder and delight.

So wander these paths with care,
Let your heart find its song,
For in this realm of enchantment,
You'll find where you belong.

Whispers of the Forgotten Trails

Beneath the canopy's sigh,
Forgotten paths gently lie,
Each step a whisper, a tale,
Of wanderers, lost, grown pale.

Moss carpets the ancient stones,
Where time itself softly moans,
Footprints faded, yet they call,
To those who dare walk tall.

In the stillness, spirits dwell,
With stories only they can tell,
Past and present swirl and bind,
In these trails, secrets unwind.

Overhead, the crows unite,
Guiding through day and night,
Their caws echo old refrain,
Reminders of joy and pain.

So tread with respect, my dear,
For the memories linger near,
In whispers soft, they convey,
The magic of yesterday.

Flights of Fancy Above the World

High above in skies so blue,
Dreams take wing, and hopes renew,
With every beat of a heart,
The journey begins, a fresh start.

Clouds like castles in the air,
Invite us to wander and dare,
To leap into the vast unknown,
Where wild adventures are grown.

With the sun as our guiding light,
We chase the day, embrace the night,
Stars sprinkle wisdom from above,
Fueling our flights with pure love.

On zephyrs soft, we shall glide,
With courage and dreams as our guide,
So spread your wings, let them fly,
For the world is yours, reach for the sky.

In the dance of the winds so free,
Find your spirit, let it be,
For in flights of fancy we weave,
The magic of dreams we believe.

The Legend of the Hidden Vale

In a vale that lies concealed,
Where ancient secrets are revealed,
Nature cradles her soft embrace,
Time flows gently, leaving no trace.

Whispers of legends float on air,
Guardians of treasures beyond compare,
A river sings to stones arrayed,
Echoes of a past that won't fade.

Beneath the stars' unblinking gaze,
The vale guards its mystic ways,
In twilight's glow, stories unfold,
Of brave hearts and treasures untold.

With every step through the glen,
The air is thick with magic then,
For in this place, dreams intertwine,
Binding the souls of yours and mine.

So if fortune guides your quest,
Seek the vale, and you'll be blessed,
For in its heart, you'll find the key,
To a world where you are free.

Whirls of Wind from Forbidden Peaks

Whirls of wind through shadows creep,
From heights where ancient secrets sleep.
Whispers call in the chilling air,
Of distant realms, the brave must dare.

Veils of mist, like dreams take flight,
Guide the wanderers through the night.
With each step, the heart does race,
In the wild, both time and space.

The mountains sigh a haunting song,
Where echoes linger, fierce and strong.
Beneath the stars that brightly shine,
Lies magic wrapped in the divine.

Footprints trace where legends bide,
Lost in time, where myths reside.
Brave souls venture, their spirits bold,
To unearth the stories long untold.

As night descends, the wind will wail,
A fleeting song, a wandering tale.
In each gust, the world will spin,
And in the heart, the quest begins.

Radiance Beyond the Jagged Edge

Beyond the jagged edge we peer,
To realms where hope and dreams draw near.
With every step upon the stone,
We chase the light, no longer lone.

The twilight paints the sky with gold,
A canvas where new tales unfold.
A shimmering path awaits the bold,
In whispers soft, the stars are told.

Through caverns deep, where shadows lie,
We seek the spark that lights the sky.
In the folds of night, the secrets keep,
While ancient guardians wake from sleep.

The journey twists, the way unknown,
Yet courage blooms, like wildflowers grown.
For in the light of spirits bright,
We find our way, we own the night.

A flicker here, a gleam above,
Guiding lost hearts to peace and love.
No jagged edge can dim the fire,
For radiant dreams are our desire.

The Pursuit of the Celestial Beasts

In the twilight's grasp, they weave and glide,
With nimble grace, through heavens wide.
The celestial beasts, with fur aflame,
In each heart beats the wildest claim.

Through the dance of stars, they lead the chase,
In silent air, we find our place.
With every leap, the skies ignite,
In dazzling dreams of dark and light.

A whisper lingers on the breeze,
Of hidden worlds, they softly tease.
We follow trails of dust and light,
To claim our place among the night.

Their laughter echoes, sweet and wild,
In every heart, we are beguiled.
To chasing shadows, we are sworn,
In the pursuit, new dreams are born.

So we shall run, through fields of stars,
Defying fear, embracing scars.
The celestial beasts, in flight so free,
Will guide our souls to destiny.

Starlight Shadows Over Untrodden Paths

In starlight shadows, secrets lie,
Where untrodden paths hold dreams that fly.
Each step a whisper, a tale untold,
In moonlit trails, our hearts behold.

Through woods enchanted, we dare to roam,
Where echoes call, we find our home.
With every turn, new wonders bloom,
In shadows deep, dispelling gloom.

The night unfurls its magic veil,
As laughter mingles with the gale.
In flickering light, we chase the past,
With every heartbeat, the die is cast.

The path unknown can raise a fear,
Yet in each shadow, a light draws near.
With courage worn like rich brocade,
We face the night, unafraid.

So let us wander through this land,
With open hearts and dreams so grand.
For in the starlight's gentle grasp,
We'll find the magic that we clasp.

Enchantment in the Glistening Air

In the glimmering mist of dawn's embrace,
Magic stirs softly in every space.
Whispers of wonder float on the breeze,
Dancing like shadows among the trees.

With a flicker of light, the fairies ignite,
Colors that shimmer, so bold and so bright.
An orchestra hums through the fluttering leaves,
Each note a promise, as daylight weaves.

The dawn sings a song of beginnings anew,
Where dreams take flight, and the skies are so blue.
In the heart of this realm, pure joy's at play,
Enchanting the world in a magical way.

Beneath the old oak, where secrets reside,
Fables and tales in the shadows abide.
Nature's soft laughter, a symphony sweet,
Echoes in harmony, where earth and dreams meet.

As the day unfolds in its radiant hue,
The enchantment whispers, forever true.
In the glistening air, the magic is clear,
A tapestry woven, as wide as the sphere.

Heartstrings Tied to the Summit

At the peak where the earth meets the sky,
Whispers of dreams on the winds flutter by.
Each step of the journey, a tale to unfold,
Heartstrings are woven with threads of pure gold.

Beneath the vast heavens, the stars seem to sigh,
Echoes of mountains that rise ever high.
In this place of wonder, where spirits unite,
The summit holds secrets, bathed in sweet light.

As the sun dips low, painting skies of deep red,
The heart learns to listen to words left unsaid.
Each heartbeat a pulse, a rhythm so true,
Connected to nature, to me and to you.

The breeze carries stories from ages long past,
Of wanderers bold who found peace at last.
With every deep breath, we drink in the air,
The heartbeat of mountains, so timeless, so rare.

Here at the summit, where dreams take their flight,
Our hearts are united in the fading light.
For in every whisper, each star's gentle gleam,
We find in this moment, the truth of our dream.

The Call of the Whispering Peaks

In the hush of the night, the peaks start to sigh,
Voices of ancient ones echo the sky.
Their whispers invite those who dare to explore,
To venture beyond to the mountains' great door.

With a heart full of courage and dreams held so tight,
We follow the call of the stars shining bright.
Guided by moonlight that dances on stone,
The summits awaken, and we are not alone.

Each step on the path tells a story of old,
Of nature's fierce magic, of legends retold.
In shadows that linger, the past intertwines,
And the whispering peaks weave their intricate lines.

The air thick with echoes of ages gone by,
The spirits of mountains, they laugh and they cry.
In their murmurs, we find the strength to be brave,
To delve into mysteries, our fears we must save.

So we climb ever higher, through darkness and light,
The call of the peaks guides our hearts through the night.
For in every whisper, a promise awaits,
To find our place boldly, unlocking the gates.

Visions Beneath the Starlit Canopy

Under the blanket of twinkling stars,
We lie on the grass with our hearts open far.
Visions emerge in the soft silver glow,
Stories unfolding, like rivers that flow.

The night tells its secrets to those brave enough,
To listen for wonders where life can be tough.
With each shooting star that dances above,
We capture the magic, the essence of love.

Fables arise from the depths of our dreams,
Whispering softly, or so it may seem.
In shadows and light, the cosmos reveals,
The truth of our hearts, and the magic that heals.

As we wander the pathways of starlit delight,
Our spirits entwined, in the infinite night.
Each flicker a promise, each sparkle a scheme,
Beneath the vast heavens, we chase every dream.

And as dawn approaches with hues of soft gold,
We carry the visions, the stories retold.
For beneath the starlit canopy high,
We find the connections that never could die.

Crags and Dreams Beneath the Moon

In the crags where shadows play,
Whispers echo through the night.
Stars above begin to sway,
Shimmering with silvery light.

Dreams take flight on moonlit beams,
Casting spells of hope and glee.
Beneath the sky, a world redeems,
Enchanting all who dare to see.

Misty trails weave through the stone,
Guiding hearts to secrets old.
With a sigh, the night has grown,
Ancient tales in silence told.

Listen close to the night's soft song,
Carried on a gentle breeze.
In this place where souls belong,
Nature's magic aims to please.

So let your dreams take root and rise,
As the world seems to embrace.
In the crags 'neath starry skies,
Find your heart, your rightful place.

The Song of Untamed Forests

In untamed forests dark and deep,
Nature hums a gentle tune.
Secrets held in shadows creep,
Beneath the watchful, silver moon.

Leaves sway softly, branches bend,
In harmony with wind's soft sigh.
Every note a timeless friend,
Singing where the spirits fly.

Murmurs echo, lifetimes spun,
In each grove, a tale unfolds.
From dawn till dusk, 'til day is done,
Every whisper touch the bold.

Creatures tread on paths well worn,
In the dance of life's embrace.
From every dusk, a new day born,
In nature's arms, we've found our place.

So let the song of forests ring,
Through the heart, it finds a way.
In each note, the wild they bring,
A timeless call to those who stay.